THE Jake COLLECTION

THE Jake COLLECTION

Annette Butterworth

ILLUSTRATED BY
NICK BUTTERWORTH

Hodder Children's Books

a division of Hodder Headline plc

Text and illustrations copyright © Annette and
Nick Butterworth, 1995,
1996 and 1998

Jake first published in Great Britain in hardback 1995
and in paperback 1996 by Hodder Children's Books

Jake Again first published in Great Britain in hardback in 1996
and in paperback in 1997 by Hodder Children's Books

Jake in Trouble first published in hardback and in paperback in 1998
by Hodder Children's Books

This bind-up edition of *Jake*, *Jake Again* and *Jake in Trouble*, first published by
Hodder Children's Books 1998

The right of Annette and Nick Butterworth to be identified as the Author
and Illustrator of the Work has been asserted by them in accordance
with the Copyright, Designs and Patents Act 1988.

10 9 8 7 6 5 4 3 2 1

All rights reserved. No part of this publication may be
reproduced, stored in a retrieval system, or transmitted,
in any form or by any means without the prior written
permission of the publisher, nor be otherwise circulated in
any form of binding or cover other than that in which it is
published and without a similar condition being
imposed on the subsequent purchaser.

All characters in this publication are fictitious
and any resemblance to real persons, living or dead,
is purely coincidental.

A Catalogue record for this book is available
from the British Library

ISBN 0340 72292 4

Printed and bound in Great Britain by
Mackays of Chatham plc, Chatham, Kent

Hodder Children's Books
A Division of Hodder Headline plc
338 Euston Road
London NW1 3BH

For Fiona
Without your enthusiasm
and vision there may not
have been three books
to collect!

Contents

Jake 3

Jake Again 63

Jake in Trouble 121

Jake

Chapter One

Jake was a bad dog. He knew he was. Sometimes he tried to be good but it was no use.

He loved to chase the ducks in the park. He would sneak up behind them when they were dozing. Then he would bark loudly and watch, as they rushed for the safety of the lake, complaining noisily.

Jake couldn't resist the smell of the dirty washing. Whenever it was being sorted out, he just had to play with it. Then he would leave it lying all over the house.

He had to roll in the sheep's droppings on the common. He liked the smell. Besides, he needed to smell like a sheep if he was going to creep up on them and round them up.

Then there was food. Or more particularly, chocolate. No chocolate was safe if Jake could reach it. Once he ate fourteen chocolate cream eggs, one after the other. He was sorry afterwards, especially as they made him ill, but he just couldn't resist them.

He couldn't help being bad.

Of course, Jake wanted to be good. He would have liked to be like those clever dogs he saw on the television. He did try to do as he was told, but it was so difficult when there always seemed to be something that needed to be chased or ripped or chewed.

He wanted to be like Holly, the dog

who lived next door. Holly was Jake's friend. She was a Rough Collie, like Lassie. She was good and she was also very beautiful. Holly had even been to Crufts.

Crufts! The biggest and best dog show in the world! Of all the reasons to be good, this was surely the most important. Only the best dogs went to Crufts. Holly had told Jake all about it. It sounded like heaven.

Crufts! Even the name sounded like a delicious kind of dog biscuit. Jake longed to see Crufts for himself. He wasn't really sure what it was like, but he thought there must be lots of chocolate there. Perhaps it was made of chocolate. Really heavenly!

Holly had told Jake how exciting it was to visit Crufts. Wonderful smells! Large halls with banners hanging from the ceilings and wide green carpet everywhere, perfect for rolling on. In the middle, a big open space called the Main Ring, where the clever dogs would show off their agility and obedience tricks. The top dogs gathered in the Main Ring to decide who was the best of the lot.

Holly said to Jake that she would love to be chosen one day, but was sure she wasn't good enough. Jake was very sure she was good enough, and loyally, and loudly, told her so.

Jake liked the sound of all the different stands with lots of food on them, especially the free samples that Holly talked about!

But most of all, Jake loved to hear about all the dogs. Thousands of them, according to Holly. All different shapes and sizes from all over the world. Australia, America, Alaska even, France, Germany, Belgium. Belgium. Jake thought his grandad came from Belgium and he liked the idea of meeting his long lost relatives.

Holly had met one dog from Alaska. She didn't know where Alaska was but she thought it must be cold because the dog had a huge thick coat of fur and said that his father used to pull a sledge.

All this talk of Crufts made Jake very excited. He told Holly he would go with her next year on her wonderful visit to Crufts.

But Jake was in for a disappointment. Sadly, Holly told Jake that a dog has to be a pedigree and specially chosen to go to Crufts. The only other dogs there are the very clever ones in the obedience competition. Holly gently told Jake that he would not be allowed into Crufts.

Charles, the Irish Wolfhound who lived on the other side of Jake's garden, laughed. Of course they wouldn't let riffraff like Jake into Crufts. It was unusual for Charles to bring himself to speak to Jake at all, because Charles thought himself very grand. His father had been the mascot for a regiment in the British Army and had told Charles not to mix with riffraff. To Charles, a mongrel like Jake was riffraff. Charles spent his time ignoring Jake's efforts to be friends.

But if Jake wasn't good, he wasn't stupid. There were lots of things that he could do. He could let himself in from the garden, for instance. He would simply jump up at the door handle and pull it down. The door would swing open and in he would go. But instead of his owners, Mr and Mrs Foster, being pleased, they were more likely to shout at Jake for scratching the door.

In the summer time, when one of the upstairs windows was open, Jake could hang out of it and see right to the end of the street. He thought he was very clever but even Jake had to admit, it wasn't clever enough for Crufts.

One of his best tricks was to pick up a big balloon without bursting it. It had taken him a long time to work this out, but one Christmas, when there'd been lots of balloons left lying about the floor, he'd had plenty to practise on. After he'd burst eleven of them, he discovered that he could pick them up from one end by

the knot. Jake proudly walked around with one for quite some time before he received the applause he was after. Then his owners found the other burst balloons. And once again he was told off.

So Jake knew he wasn't good. He'd certainly been told enough times. The

Crufts obedience competition was just out of the question. And, although he did think that he was quite handsome, he knew he wasn't a pedigree.

Jake had to accept that the one thing he wanted more than anything else, to go to Crufts, would never happen.

Chapter Two

At the bottom of Jake's garden, there was a gap in the hedge that he could squeeze through. On the other side, there lay an overgrown wilderness of a garden, which, to Jake, was the only kind of garden worth having. One corner of this garden that he particularly liked had a pond with frogs in it. Jake liked to wait by the pond until the frogs started jumping. Then he would startle them by leaping on them and chasing them. Jake thought this was a terrific game. The frogs weren't so sure.

It was in the middle of one of these games that Jake met Sam. Since then, Sam had become Jake's favourite person.

Sam lived in a ramshackle house that stood in the wilderness of a garden. He was no longer a young man. He'd moved to England a long time ago from his home in Belgium. Unfortunately, he had always found it difficult to speak English and he had very few friends and no relations in England. He was a lonely man.

Until he met Jake.

Sam understood Jake and Jake understood Sam. Sam knew that Jake was a loyal dog who had unusual abilities. Jake knew that Sam was a kind man who didn't mind where he dug in the garden and would always share his sandwiches. Jake loved the smell of Sam. It reminded him of the dirty washing he liked to play with. It pleased Jake that Sam was from Belgium. Maybe Sam knew his grandad. Jake and Sam became firm friends. Sam asked Mr and Mrs Foster if he could take Jake for walks, and now it was nearly always Sam who took Jake out.

One morning Jake squeezed through the hedge to find Sam sitting outside, feeding the birds. Jake knew he had to be very quiet until Sam had finished. Sam didn't like the birds to be frightened. Jake wanted to chase them off but he kept still for Sam.

When the birds had gone, he moved up to sit next to Sam and nuzzled at his hand. Jake was feeling very disappointed this morning because Holly had told him that her owners had entered her again in the Crufts competition. He would have loved to watch her there.

"Hallo, old boy," said Sam to Jake. "How you doing? You don't seem to be your old bouncy self this morning. Tell you what, Sam will take you for a nice walk."

Sam could always talk more easily to Jake because he didn't worry about how he sounded. Jake's ears pricked up at the suggestion of a walk. Their favourite park was only five minutes away. Soon Sam and Jake were walking through the big, green, park gates.

Jake rushed everywhere,

checking up on things. There were a few squirrels who needed chasing up a tree and some ducks that needed putting in their place. Sam let him get on with it: he knew Jake didn't mean any harm. The animals were used to him.

They made their way through the park until they came to the football pitch where Jake began to nuzzle at an old carrier bag that Sam was carrying.

"All right, boy, steady on. I know what you want. Give me a chance!" Sam reached into the bag and pulled out a football that he always brought with him.

"O.K. Jake. Let's have a game."

At the sight of the ball, Jake leapt into the air and ran round and round in circles until the game began.

Jake was really marvellous with a football. He dribbled the ball back to Sam right from the other end of the pitch. Sam kicked the ball into the air and Jake headed it a few times with his long muzzle. Then he trapped it with his front legs and dribbled it back with his nose.

As Jake got more excited, he crept closer and closer as Sam was trying to kick the ball. Sam shouted, "Ten yards! Ten yards!" and Jake backed away until Sam was satisfied he was far enough away not to get kicked.

People would often gather to watch Sam and Jake. They were amazed that a dog could be so clever with a ball. Sadly for Jake, even being able to play football didn't qualify a dog for Crufts.

Today, there was a football match being played on the pitch next to Jake and Sam's. Before Sam realised it, Jake had disappeared.

"Where has he gone?" thought Sam.

Suddenly, Sam looked across at the

football pitch next to him and saw Jake right in the middle of it! He'd decided to join in a proper game of football. Jake was rushing along the pitch, nudging the football with his muzzle and beating everybody in sight. Both teams of footballers chased after him but nobody was quick enough to catch Jake.

He rushed around the pitch, causing havoc and was enjoying himself so much that he didn't hear Sam's frantic shouts to come back and leave the ball.

One after the other, the footballers tried to get their ball back. It was no use. Jake was too quick and the pitch too muddy.

The footballers were furious. Their match was ruined.

Jake couldn't understand why everybody was so upset. Surely, they'd had a lovely time. A good chase and all that mud. But even Sam was cross with him, and he was led home in disgrace.

Chapter Three

Sam couldn't stay cross with Jake for long. Jake looked so upset at not being friends that the next day, Sam and Jake went to the park as usual.

Today, the park was quite deserted except for a couple of shifty-looking boys. They seemed to be on the look out for trouble. They watched as Sam put Jake through his paces.

"O.K. Jake. It's nice and quiet today. Let's go!" Sam kicked the ball high into the air. Jake waited in just the right spot for the ball to come down and before it touched the ground, he bounced it off his muzzle, not once, but three times! Then he dribbled the ball back to Sam, and placed it right at Sam's feet.

Sam gave the ball another mighty kick. Jake rushed away after it, but at that moment, one of the watching boys stepped forward and caught the ball. Then he pulled something from his pocket. It was long, shiny and very sharp. It was a knife! The boy stabbed the ball. The ball instantly burst.

"Won't be able to do your tricks now!" he sneered and he kicked out at Jake.

Sam wasn't bothered about the ball but seeing this thug kick out at Jake made his blood boil. He marched up to the boy and took him by the scruff of the neck. The boy was so taken aback that he dropped his knife.

"Now then, you bully, you pick on someone your own size and leave a dumb animal alone," said Sam.

He let go of the boy and, shaking, put Jake on his lead and took him home.

When Jake and Sam arrived back at Jake's house, Jake's owner answered the door.

"My goodness, are you all right, Mr Haagen? You look so pale! It wasn't Jake, was it? Was he a bad boy again?" Mrs Foster asked.

"No, no, he's never a bad dog. No, it was nothing, it's all sorted out."

"Would you like a cup of tea?" asked Mrs Foster.

"No thank you, I'm perfectly all right."

Really Sam would have liked a cup of tea but he was too shy to accept.

When Sam had gone home, Jake had his dinner then a nap. When he woke up he went out into the garden to see Holly.

Excitedly he told his friend all that had happened in the park.

Holly was anxious to know if Jake was all right. She was worried about Sam as well but Jake told her that Sam had been wonderful, a real hero. He added that, if he had had the chance, he would have seen the boys off. Holly smiled. Jake liked to boast about what he could do. Holly often wondered what he really could do!

Holly could hear her owner calling her in for the night, so she gave Jake a friendly nuzzle through the fence and left him on his own.

Jake strolled around his garden for a little while, checking up on things. When he reached the hole into Sam's garden, he thought he'd just pop through to check out the frogs. They were always very lively at this time of night.

As Jake reached the pond, he was surprised to hear the sound of shouting. It seemed to be coming from the direction of Sam's back door.

Jake didn't like the shouting. He sensed

that something was wrong.

He rushed towards the back door, then saw a horrible sight. Two boys were pushing Sam backwards and forwards between them. They were pushing harder and harder. Sam was shouting at them to stop but this just made them push even more. They pushed Sam so hard that he fell to the ground.

Horrified, Jake saw one of the boys take something from his pocket. Jake's hackles rose. He remembered the burst football.

These thugs were the boys from the park. They'd come to get their own back on Sam. But they had reckoned without Jake.

With a ferocious snarl, Jake flew at the boy with the knife and grabbed his arm in his powerful jaws, forcing him to the ground. The boys were totally taken by surprise. The one on the ground was helpless. Jake pinned him down hard. The other one started kicking at Jake, trying to make him let go.

The kicks hurt Jake dreadfully. He yelped, but he would not let go. He knew it was the only chance Sam had to get help. Sam picked himself up and stumbled into the house to telephone the police. At that moment, the thug who was kicking at Jake decided to run for it.

When Sam came back, the boy with the knife was still on the ground with Jake on top of him, his long muzzle pushed into the boy's face. Jake held the boy down with his legs. He snarled at the boy if he tried to move. Jake seemed like a different dog from the one who'd played football in the park. His claws were very sharp, his teeth looked deadly and his eyes menacing.

The police seemed to be a very long time and Sam began to wonder if they would ever come. But Jake didn't move. He held the boy down the whole time. When the police arrived, two of them rushed in and grabbed the boy on the ground. Only then did Jake let go.

"Well, well, look who it is," said one of the policeman. "It's Eddie Price. Well done, dog. You've caught a very nasty villain! Last week, these two boys hurt an old lady so badly that she's still recovering in hospital. Bullies, that's what they are. Thanks to this dog, *he* won't be bullying anybody else and we'll soon find his pal."

Sam rushed over to Jake to see if he was all right. Jake felt very sore and bruised from the kicking and, in particular, his right back leg felt very stiff.

The neighbours had heard the sound of the police cars arriving. Most had rushed out into the street, others were peering through the curtains. Soon, it seemed that half the street was arriving in Sam's garden, including Jake's owners and Holly. As the story of what had happened became clear, everyone agreed that the hero of the day was Jake.

"What a marvellous dog!" they said.

"What a brave dog! Saved Sam's life, I don't doubt."

"Always knew he was an unusual dog!"

Jake couldn't really understand why they were making so much fuss. He loved Sam and he couldn't bear to see him hurt. It was as simple as that. Still, it was rather nice to be told that he had done something right for a change!

Chapter Four

In the days following the attack on Sam, Jake became quite a celebrity. The local newspaper sent a reporter to interview Sam and Jake's owners.

At first, Sam wasn't very keen on this because it meant that he had to speak. Jake's owners helped him and gradually Sam actually began to enjoy talking to people. He found he knew more English than he thought. A new friendship developed between the Foster family and their neighbour Sam.

As for Jake, he loved every minute of it. He always enjoyed attention and he posed happily for the newspaper photographer who thought that Jake was a perfect model. He had taken quite a few pictures in the garden when suddenly, Jake pricked up his ears. He'd heard the sound of the washing machine door being opened. While Mr Foster was busy talking to the photographer, Jake sneaked off into the house to help sort out the dirty washing.

After a while, Mr Foster and the photographer noticed that Jake had disappeared.

"Come on, Jake! Here boy!" Mr Foster called. "We just need a couple more."

Jake's head appeared round the corner of the back door with a pair of Mr Foster's underpants wrapped around it. That very second, the photographer's camera flashed. Next morning, Jake appeared in the newspapers wearing a rather unusual hat!

Mrs Foster read out the newspaper headline over breakfast.

"Wonder dog tames attacker," she said proudly. "That's our Jake!" and she chuckled at the photograph.

Holly was thrilled. At last her friend was receiving the attention she thought he deserved. She told Jake that she was very proud of him. He was quite right, he had indeed 'seen them off'! She'd seen his picture on the front page of the newspapers.

Jake pretended that he thought everybody was making a big fuss. But secretly he was very pleased to suddenly be so popular.

There was one thing, though, that did bother Jake. His leg, which had been so cruelly kicked by the thug, was still very stiff. He couldn't walk without limping.

The day after the attack, he was taken to the vets, which he hated. He always hated the vets. He hated the smells and he hated having to sit on that table. He didn't hate the vet though, who seemed quite nice. The vet gave Jake a thorough examination.

"Well, Mrs Foster, I don't think Jake has come to any real harm from his brave ordeal. I'm not so sure about this leg though. I think it's dislocated and although it will heal, he may be left with a limp."

Jake didn't like that idea. He liked to be able to charge about everywhere and a limp would really slow him down. "Well," he thought. "It was a small price

to pay to save Sam from being hurt."

Next day, Charles, the Irish Wolfhound, began to take Jake in hand. Charles went up to Jake now and gave him a friendly nudge with his huge head.

Charles realised that his old father had been wrong. He was forced to admit that it didn't matter what a dog looked like. It was how he behaved that counted.

Holly stood by and beamed at the pair of them. She didn't like it when people weren't friendly to one another so she

was thrilled to see Charles accepting Jake at last.

Charles decided to teach Jake to march properly, like his old father. He was sure Jake's limp would not seem half so bad. Charles assured Jake that he would have him fit for duty in any army in no time!

And so daily lessons with Charles, the gentle giant, began, with tips from Holly.

The first lesson Jake learned from Charles was how to stand smartly to attention. Charles stood proudly, chest out, head held high, legs straight and tail down. Jake tried to copy him.

Holly called out from her garden that this was how she had to stand in the show ring, and Charles agreed.

Charles began to show Jake how to place his feet slowly and deliberately, two legs at a time, on opposite sides, so that they moved in perfect harmony. Holly thought what a comical couple they made: the proud Charles striding out and the limping Jake following behind as best he could. But she didn't laugh, not so much as a titter. She wouldn't have dreamed of hurting their feelings.

After the first lesson, Jake crawled through the fence to Sam's garden.

Sam was feeding his birds, so Jake waited quietly.

"Hallo boy, how's your poor old leg? Come here, let Sam rub it for you," and

Sam soothed Jake's injured leg, and made it feel easier. "When your leg is better Jake, we'll go to the park again. I've got a new ball."

Jake nuzzled at Sam's hand. He was quiet and not his boisterous self. He wondered if his leg would ever get better. He hoped so.

Chapter Five

After some time, the fuss over Jake died down. Jake began to get used to the shorter and colder days as autumn gave way to winter. The vet gave permission for Jake to be taken for his walks again. The weather was not very good, so Sam only took him out occasionally and Jake's footballing skills were becoming a little rusty. And he still had a slight limp.

One day, Jake squeezed through the

hedge into Sam's garden and barked outside Sam's door to let him know he had arrived. Sam let him into the kitchen. To Jake's surprise, instead of the usual welcome dog biscuit, Sam gave him a big piece of Belgian chocolate.

"I shouldn't really give you this, Jakie, but I think you deserve it today," said Sam. "In my paper, it says they've put those two thugs in prison for a good long time. The poor old lady they attacked is in hospital." Sam thought for a moment. "They could have done the same to me if it hadn't been for you," he said, and he hugged Jake.

The pair of them went to the park and although Jake was a little slower, he still played football.

As Jake was dribbling the ball back to Sam, he found a rather nice patch of fox's dung and so he decided to roll in it. To his surprise Sam shouted at him to stop. "Not today, Jake. Got to smell your best!"

Jake wondered what Sam meant. He didn't usually stop him rolling. Besides, if he needed to smell his best, surely he had better carry on rolling! But he didn't. He always tried to do what Sam said.

When Jake and Sam arrived at Jake's house, Mrs Foster had a cup of tea waiting for Sam. Sam always had a cup of tea with her these days.

Jake was pleased. He wanted Sam to see where he slept. He was very proud of

his present cardboard box. Jake's owners had once bought him a proper dog basket but he'd never slept in it, preferring to stick to his cardboard box. So they had given up and now they just kept replacing the boxes. He'd been working on this one since it arrived as a replacement for his last one and he felt it was now just about perfect. Of course, it wouldn't stay like that, they never did. They seemed to quickly lose their shape.

Today Sam wasn't paying attention. "I tried to stop him rolling, Mrs Foster, but you know what he is," he said.

"Oh, don't worry, Sam. I'm going to sort him out later," replied Mrs Foster.

"Well, I'll be going then. See you soon. Bye Jake, see you boy."

Jake was worried. What did Mrs Foster mean when she said, "I'm going to sort him out later?" It didn't sound too good.

It sounded horribly like a bath was on its way. Jake decided that he'd better lie low. For the rest of the day, Jake stayed out of the way, in case he was right.

That night, Jake heard the sound he dreaded – the sound of the bath water running. And he could smell that awful stuff they put in the water. As soon as he saw Mrs Foster's plastic apron, he knew the worst was about to happen. He was to be bathed.

How could they do it? It had taken him ages to work up the smell he had now and he was particularly pleased with it. Weeks of work washed down the plug hole in minutes!

"Besides," thought Jake, "it's crazy in this weather. It's freezing cold."

Straightaway, Jake put his bath plan into action. He followed this whenever he was threatened with a bath. His aim was to make life as difficult as possible for the person giving him the bath.

First, Jake made himself scarce. If Mrs Foster couldn't find him then she couldn't bath him.

This time, when Mrs Foster tracked him down, she found him squeezed under the spare bed. Jake hadn't hidden there since he was a puppy. When he tried to get out, he remembered *why*. It was really much too small for him now, Mrs Foster had to lift the bed up to get him out.

If he couldn't actually avoid being put into the bath, the second part of Jake's bath plan was never to keep still whilst in the water. First he sat down, then he jumped up and turned himself round and round and round until he made himself dizzy. After that he had to keep still, and so Mrs Foster managed to clean him up.

Finally, Jake would try to make as much mess as he could when he stepped out of the bath. If he was wet, then he made sure everybody else got wet too. This time, he shook himself before Mrs Foster could get the towel on him. He soaked her, the floor, the walls and all the dry towels hanging by the bath.

"That was a good one!" thought Jake.

"I won!"

He expected to be scolded and he was surprised that Mrs Foster wasn't more cross. She only told him off lightly. Jake was actually a bit disappointed.

"This is odd," thought Jake. "A bath in mid-winter, a thorough soaking and all she says is 'Oh Jake'. There's something funny going on."

After his bath, Jake was given his supper and allowed to lie in front of the fire to dry off. As he went to sleep that night, he actually felt rather comfortable. He had to admit to himself that perhaps, just occasionally, a bath wasn't so bad after all.

Just occasionally, mind.

Chapter Six

The following day, Jake was surprised to find everybody up and about before he was properly awake. It was still dark. Jake climbed out of his box and stretched his early morning stretch. He trotted up to greet Mrs Foster, as usual, as she entered the kitchen, only to get another surprise.

Mrs Foster was already dressed and wearing clothes that Jake had only seen her wear on special occasions.

"Morning, Jakie. Oh good, you still look smart. Come here, let's give you a final brush up."

"A final brush up! You're joking!" thought Jake.

Although he had been taken by surprise and was still a bit dozy, Jake immediately fell to the floor and lay down, flat out. As he lay there, Mrs Foster brushed what she could. Eventually and rather reluctantly, Jake stood up for her.

"What is this all about?" thought Jake. "Oh, I know. We're going to visit her mother. She doesn't like me much. She doesn't like the way I smell. I hope it's not for long. I'd better say goodbye to Holly and Sam before we go. I hope they're up."

After the grooming, Jake was allowed out into the garden for some last minute checks. To his surprise, everything was quiet next door in Holly's garden. Sam was not about either, but it was a bit early for him. Jake heard his owners calling and he knew that this meant the beginning of a long boring journey.

Jake jumped into the car and prepared himself for several sleeps. He was surprised to see that even Mr Foster was all dressed up. He looked rather uncomfortable in his suit.

Jake was right. The journey lasted about five sleeps. A long one. That meant no more walks with Sam for a while.

At long last, as the car began to slow down, Jake sat up to see what was happening. The car was pulling into a great big concrete car park. There were lots of other cars there, many of them with pictures of dogs on them.

"Well, this is odd," thought Jake. "Are we stopping for a drink?"

Mr and Mrs Foster got out of the car but there were no drinks in sight. Jake had his lead put on and he jumped out.

"I think this is the way," said Mrs Foster. "Anyway, I've got the passes, so we can go in anywhere."

Jake trotted along beside them, feeling more and more puzzled.

After they'd walked for five minutes, Jake saw a very large building looming up in front of them. He couldn't understand the writing on it but it seemed like an important building. When they reached one of the side doors, Mrs Foster handed some pieces of paper to a man.

"Oh good, I'm so glad you've made it. So pleased to meet you at last."

"I think he means me," thought Jake.

When Jake stepped inside the building, he knew where he was at once.

He had dreamed about it so much.

He was at Crufts.

Crufts! He could hardly believe it.

He took a deep breath and smelt all the delicious smells. It was just as Holly had described it. The banners. The big green carpets. But most of all, the dogs!

Everywhere he looked there were dogs. Tall dogs, small dogs, some very hairy dogs, others nearly bald! Some dogs barked excitedly to each other, whilst others sat patiently on wooden benches. In his whole life, Jake had never seen so many dogs. He stood gazing at everything around him with a wonderful expression of contentment on his face.

So, this was Crufts. At last!

A man with a badge came to meet Jake and his owners. He took them to have a cup of tea and some biscuits and a drink of water for Jake.

"Now, I expect you would like to have a look round first, wouldn't you?" said the Crufts man. "That's fine, but please make sure you're back here in time."

So off they went for a good look around.

Jake met the dogs that pulled sledges. They were called Alaskan Malamutes.

He talked with some dogs called Great Danes who were nearly as big as Charles, and he met some Chihuahuas from

Mexico that were so small that he nearly trod on one!

Jake had been talking to one dog for nearly five minutes before he realised he was talking to its tail, not its head!

Some dogs had such fancy haircuts that Jake thought they looked more like hedges than dogs.

Jake met the Belgian Shepherd dogs. These, he thought, were the most handsome of all the dogs. Perhaps because they looked a bit like him.

"Just like my grandad!" he thought.

As Jake walked amongst the food stalls,

he was given so many tit-bits that even he began to feel full.

Everybody seemed to know who he was and wanted to make a fuss of him. Jake thought it was wonderful.

Eventually, the Fosters and Jake arrived back where they had started.

The Crufts man was waiting for them.

"Right," he said, "here's somebody I think you know. He's been having lunch with us," and to Jake's surprise and joy, there was Sam, standing in front of him!

Sam was wearing an outfit like Mr Foster's and he didn't smell like Sam at all. Obviously poor Sam had been forced to have a bath as well and have his hair combed. Jake jumped up at him and even though he was so dressed up, Sam didn't mind a bit.

"Jakie! Lovely to see you boy," said Sam.

"Well now, is everybody ready?" said the Crufts man briskly. "Then let's go."

Sam took Jake by the lead, and Jake found himself in a fenced off area with several other dogs.

"These other dogs will be coming in after you. We'd like Jake to lead our parade of heroes," the Crufts man said to Sam.

It was only then that Jake realised what was about to happen. He was about to go into the Main Ring at Cruft's Dog Show!

Sam and Jake waited at the entrance to the ring, next to a large arrangement of flowers. Jake sniffed at the flowers and wrinkled his nose. He never could stand the smell of roses. He got up and moved towards them, but suddenly Sam was leading him into that great big green open space called the Main Ring!

All around the ring sat a huge crowd of

people. As soon as they caught sight of Jake and Sam, they clapped and cheered.

Then a loud voice said, "And leading our parade is Jake, owned by Mr and Mrs Foster and accompanied by Mr Sam Haagen. Jake is to receive our award for exceptional bravery for saving Mr Haagen from a terribly violent attack."

Sam and Jake were joined in the middle of the big ring by a very important-looking lady. She beamed at Jake and patted his head. Then, from a small table, she picked up a beautiful blue sash with silver edges and put it around Jake's neck.

She turned

to Sam and handed him a silver medal with a ribbon which matched Jake's sash. Solemnly, they shook hands and paws, then Jake and Sam did a lap of honour around the ring. Again the people clapped and cheered. Jake was very glad that he'd had lessons from Charles. He stuck out his chest proudly as he trotted round. There was no sign of a limp.

Suddenly, Jake caught sight of Holly. She was standing over in a corner. As he passed, he couldn't resist stopping to talk to her. Holly told Jake her own marvellous news. She had been chosen as the best Rough Collie and would be in the big ring later!

"Wonderful!" thought Jake. "What a *wonderful* day!"

After their lap of honour, Jake and Sam were asked to stay in the centre whilst the other dogs in the parade came in.

There were five others. One dog had woken up his mistress when their house had caught fire. Another dog had sniffed out a haul of drugs that were being smuggled into the country in fake wine bottles. There was a police dog and next to him there was a Guide dog for the Blind who were both retiring after an exceptional number of years of faithful service. Another dog had stayed with his owner after he had injured himself in a climbing accident. The dog had kept him warm and alive until the rescuers arrived.

When all the dogs were in the ring, Jake and Sam were asked to lead a final parade of honour around the ring. Jake was at the front because he had risked his own life for Sam.

Jake had made it to Crufts after all. He wasn't a pedigree, and he could never match the dogs in the obedience competition. But there was one thing that Jake hadn't known. No one had told him about the special parade for exceptional dogs. Clever dogs. Brave dogs.

And Jake had proved himself the bravest of all.

Together, Sam and Jake left the ring. As they passed by the large flower arrangement, Jake caught the heavy perfume of the roses again.

"Pooh!" he thought. And he decided to do something about them.

Without warning, Jake went over to the arrangement, cocked his leg and watered the flowers.

A chorus of voices cried out. . .

"Oh Jake!"

Jake Again

Chapter One

Jake was in disgrace. It is true he didn't know it was his owner's birthday. But he shouldn't have eaten the whole box of chocolates that was meant to be her birthday present.

When the box arrived on the doormat, Jake thought it was wonderful. Mrs Foster's sister had called and, finding the Fosters out, posted her present through the letter box. But she'd forgotten about Jake. Jake had eaten most of the chocolates, and the ones he didn't like he had left, half chewed and stuck to the carpet. Mr and

Mrs Foster came home to a terrible mess in the hall.

To make matters worse, Jake had dug up some roses that Mr Foster had just planted. They were another present. Mr Foster always sprinkled a handful of bonemeal around the roots of plants to help them grow. Jake hated the smell of roses but he loved bonemeal. So, to get to the bonemeal, he dug up the roses and spoilt Mr Foster's best efforts.

Of course, he was sorry afterwards. Jake always was.

Jake did like having a good dig. He had found some very interesting things, digging. Once, he'd found some old tools that eventually ended up in a museum. Jake wasn't impressed. He'd been hoping to find a bone to eat.

Jake went to the local park with his great friend, Sam, nearly every day. Sam was an old man who lived in a house that backed onto Jake's garden. Sam and the Fosters had become friends through Jake, and Sam took Jake for his daily walks. In the park, they would meet up with their pals; Jake with his doggy friends and Sam with their owners.

Today, Jake crawled through the hole in the fence to Sam's garden. Sam had heard about the chocolates and the roses, but he gave Jake a hug and a pat, and a dog biscuit, as he always did. Sam knew Jake was a dog who tried to be good but sometimes temptations were too much for him.

"Hallo, Jake. You are a rascal," said Sam. "I wonder why you hate roses so much. They're my favourite flowers. I am going to finish my cup of tea and then we'll try out our new football in the park."

Jake was a very good footballer. He was good at dribbling and heading the ball. Football was his favourite game.

"Let's see if I can score a goal today, Jake," said Sam.

Chapter Two

When Jake and Sam arrived at the park, Jake's friends and their owners were at the entrance.

Jake's favourite friend, Holly, a Rough Collie, was there. She lived next door to Jake. Holly had her nephew Harry staying at the moment. Holly and Harry were not as clever as Jake but they were very kind and Harry was very excited to see Jake, who was his hero. Harry wanted to look like Jake when he grew up. Holly didn't like to disappoint him by telling him he wouldn't grow up any further. Holly thought that, anyway, he was quite big enough.

Charles, the Irish Wolfhound, was standing next to his owner, Mr Grant. He gave Jake a friendly nudge. Charles lived on the other side of Jake's garden. To begin with the two had not got on, but now they were firm friends.

The dogs and their owners were gathered reading a poster on the park notice board.

They had very miserable faces.

Mrs Thirkettle, Holly's owner, greeted Sam. "Look, isn't it awful? The Council are going to sell the park!"

"Sell the park! They can't do that, can they?" Sam asked Mr Grant.

"It seems they can," said Mr Grant. "The poster says the park is to become an industrial and business park with factories and office outlets."

"That's terrible," said Sam.

The dogs understood enough to know what the notice meant. Harry wondered if a business park would still be a place where dogs could go. But Jake told him that this sort of park wasn't really a park at all. There would be no grass, no trees, no swings, no bandstand, no tennis courts, no lake, no ducks, no animals at all. And, saddest of all for Jake – no football pitch.

This was dreadful news for the dogs. If they lost their park where else could they run free, without being on a lead? Where would they meet to play their games and exchange stories?

The owners were just as upset.

"What about all the trees?" asked Mrs. Thirkettle. "I've been coming to this park for fifty years and I've seen them grow from saplings to huge, healthy, beautiful trees. They'll pull them all down."

"And there's the lake, of course," said Mr Grant. "All the fish will go, and the geese, ducks, swans, moorhens, coots. And the fishermen will have nowhere. It's just too awful."

"Who are they going to sell the park to?" asked Sam.

"That man over there," said Mr Grant. He pointed to a short fat man smoking a cigar, who was directing some workmen to take measurements.

"What are the Council thinking about?" asked Sam. The fat man with the measuring tape must have overheard. He turned and strolled towards them.

"I'll tell you what they're thinking about," he said, with an unpleasant smile. "Allow me to introduce myself. My name is Ted Griffen and I am the new owner of this park or at least, I will be very soon. The Council want to modernise this town: bring it into the modern age, bring new life to the business community of the area. By selling this park to me, that is exactly what they will be doing."

"And it hasn't got anything to do with the money they will get from the sale?" asked Mr Grant. "Everybody knows they have run out of money."

"That's nothing to do with me," replied Ted Griffen. "I've got a business to run and a living to make and if you don't mind, your dogs are getting in the way of my measuring."

Jake didn't like the man or his measuring. Without any warning, he seized hold of one of the measures and started running round in circles with it, trailing it behind him. Ted Griffen tried to catch him and ended up wrapped in the tape. Everybody was laughing – except Ted Griffen. "You just wait," he shouted. "You won't be laughing soon, when this park belongs to me."

Sam called Jake over and made him let go of the tape. "OK Jakie, that will do. We'll have to think of something else to stop this man," he said.

Sam was very sad. Without the park, there would be no more walks with his great friend Jake, and no more chats with the people there. These were the only friends Sam had. Jake could see Sam was sad. He didn't know how to save the park, but he knew he must.

The dogs and their owners drifted on through the park, but they were not their usual lively selves.

"Of course, you know, the park belongs to the people of the town," said Mrs Thirkettle. "The land was given to us by King Edward the Confessor nearly a thousand years ago! People were allowed to leave their sheep and goats here to graze. There used to be an old piece of sheepskin parchment hanging in the Town Hall. That was the Royal Charter. A very important document. The Charter said that Edward the Confessor gave the land to the town. If it hadn't gone missing, the Council wouldn't be able to sell the park."

"If only we had that Charter," said Mr Grant. "We could prove that the park belongs to the town."

"Well, I haven't seen that Charter since I was a young girl, and that's a long time ago," said Mrs Thirkettle. "But I suppose it must be somewhere."

"Then we must find it," said Sam.

The dogs were trying to understand. Jake didn't know what sheepskin parchment was, but he did know what sheep were. He had seen them on the common. He knew their smell. He thought they needed to find a piece of a sheep. Charles thought perhaps this Charter thing was a special sort of bone and the other dogs agreed. They must find a special sheep's bone and then the park would be safe.

Chapter Three

"I think this public meeting has been arranged much too quickly," Mrs Foster said to Sam. "We haven't had time to think."

They were having their morning cup of tea together after Sam and Jake's walk.

"It's only a week since the Council first put up the board about selling the park."

"That could be their idea," said Sam. "It will be harder for people to stop them if they move fast."

"What did the notice say, Sam?"

"It said that anybody interested should go to the Town Hall tonight for a meeting with the Council, to discuss the sale of the park," Sam replied.

"Such short notice," said Mrs Foster. "Sam, I think I'll take Jake along. Do you think that's a good idea?"

"Wonderful," said Sam, pleased. "Let them meet all the users of the park. And Jake is always full of surprises!"

That evening Sam, Mr and Mrs Foster and Jake arrived at the Town Hall for the public meeting. At first, the doorman refused to let Jake in.

"No dogs," he said gruffly.

"But this isn't just any dog," said Mrs Foster. "This is Jake. The Council have invited 'anybody interested' along to this meeting. And nobody is more interested in the park than Jake!"

"Oh, all right then," said the doorman, reluctantly. "But make sure he behaves himself."

Mr and Mrs Foster, Sam and Jake, found themselves some seats near the back. Mrs Foster looped Jake's lead under a chair leg and they waited for the meeting to begin.

Jake was pleased to find himself sitting behind a little girl. He liked to be made a fuss of. He was even more pleased to see the little girl had some chocolate.

At the front of the hall, on a raised platform, the Councillors sat in a row behind a long table. Ted Griffen, the developer, sat with them. The rest of the hall was packed with townsfolk. The news about the sale of the park had

spread fast and the people of the town were very upset.

"Good evening, ladies and gentlemen. I am Mr Ramsey, the Mayor and Leader of the Council. So good to see so many of you here tonight."

The Mayor, however, didn't look at all pleased to see them. In fact, the Council had hoped to keep the meeting a small and quiet affair.

The Mayor went on to explain that the Council wanted to modernise the town. They wanted to build lots of business facilities to benefit the whole town and

they were sure everybody would gain enormously from the development of the park. The Mayor spoke for ages, boring people with facts and figures.

At last he said, "Are there any questions?"

"Yes," said Mr Grant. "Without the park, where will we be able to get some fresh air and exercise? Our dogs can't run around in the streets, it's not safe. And we'll lose the trees and the lake if you allow this industrial park."

"Well," said the Mayor, "unfortunately, we will have to lose the trees in the park but most people will still be able to walk through the business park."

"And dogs?" asked Mr Foster.

"Oh no, certainly not. No animals allowed in a business park. For health and safety reasons."

"How is the sale of the park going to benefit the ordinary people of the town?" asked Mrs Foster.

"Well," said the Mayor again. He was clearly a bit stuck for an answer and looked at Mr Griffen.

"I'll tell you," interrupted Ted Griffen. "This Council needs more money for schools, roads, and hospitals. The sale of the park will raise this money."

"But why do you need more money?" asked Mrs Foster. "You usually have enough. What's happened to it all?"

"Well," said the Mayor yet again, "we have had to decorate the Council offices and, of course, we had to replace all the councillors' cars."

"The councillors can buy their own cars," said Mr Grant, "and you certainly didn't need to buy those antiques and paintings that you have got in your office."

Jake wasn't interested in what the Mayor had to say. He and the little girl had finished the chocolate ages ago. Now they were bored. They watched as a bee lazily buzzed between the chairs.

Jake lowered his head onto his paws, and sighed.

"It isn't right," said Mrs Thirkettle. "That park belongs to the people of this town. It was given to us by Edward the Confessor nearly a thousand years ago, by Royal Charter. The Charter used to be here, in the Town Hall. It gave the parkland to us, and it isn't the Council's to sell."

"Ah yes, well," said the Mayor, "that is a very old story and nobody has seen that 'Charter', if it ever existed, for years and years. If it were to be found, which is highly unlikely, we would, of course, abide by it. In the meantime, however, the Council takes the view that the park should be sold. For the benefit of the town, of course. I think we all agree then," he said, looking at the other councillors, "that unless we have another offer, we should accept Mr Griffen's generous one and sell the park to him."

Everybody, except the councillors, began to boo the Mayor. At this point, the bee buzzed past Jake's nose. He couldn't resist it. He jumped up and rushed after it, snapping at it, trying to catch it. Unfortunately, the chair, with his lead wrapped around it, went with him. Mr Foster fell onto the floor and Jake knocked over several other chairs.

Suddenly, the meeting was in uproar. People hurried to get out of Jake's way. As the bee flew past the Mayor, Jake rushed past him, knocked him over and finally caught the bee.

"Er, I think I'd better declare the meeting over," the Mayor yelled from the floor.

"Oh Jake," said Mrs Foster, as she got hold of his lead. "Why are you always so naughty?"

"But it was funny, wasn't it, to see the Mayor on the floor?" Sam laughed.

Jake was sorry that he'd pulled Mr Foster over. He had got carried away by the bee. He had to admit that he wasn't very sorry he'd knocked the Mayor over.

Chapter Four

After the meeting at the Town Hall, the people of the town knew they had to find a way to save the park.

The councillors, and especially the Mayor, were determined to sell it. They all wanted to keep their new cars. And the Mayor had taken a particular dislike to Jake.

At first, they tried to find the missing Charter. If it could be found, the park couldn't be sold.

Mr and Mrs Foster, and Sam, went to the local library to see if it was kept there. There was no sign of it. But a helpful librarian told them that Mrs Thirkettle was right. King Edward *had* given the park to the town.

Mrs Foster then wrote to several big museums in London, to see if any of them had the Charter or knew where it was. But none of them could help. She spent a whole day in one museum and found nothing.

She did wonder if the Queen knew about the Charter. After all, she must be related to King Edward. So she wrote to the Queen to ask if she had the Charter.

Mrs Foster received a letter back from her Majesty saying that she was very sorry, she had looked everywhere she could think, but she couldn't find the Charter either. She very much hoped that it would turn up in time to save the park.

"What are we going to do?" Mrs Foster said to Sam. "We can't save the park without that Charter. It must be somewhere. But where? Suppose somebody has destroyed it!"

"Don't give up hope, Mrs Foster," said Sam. "Something might turn up."

The next morning, Jake and Sam arrived at the park as usual, to find Ted Griffen and his workmen already there. They were busy, drawing up plans and painting white crosses on a group of trees which were roped off to stop people getting near them.

"The Council are letting these people cut down some trees to make room for their machines. They don't even own the park yet but they're so sure they will!" Mrs Thirkettle said. Sam knew that Mrs

Thirkettle was very fond of this group of trees.

Jake watched in horror as a workman took a large chainsaw and attacked one of the big trees.

There was a crowd of people watching and shouting. The dogs joined in by barking loudly.

"Now, stand well back, for your own safety," said Ted Griffen. "We can't cut trees down with people too close."

Sam was suddenly very angry. "You shouldn't be cutting them down at all," he shouted, and he gave Jake's football a mighty kick.

Jake thought it was time for a game. He chased after it, and began to dribble it in and out of the big oaks. He got completely in the way of the workmen.

"Call your dog off," shouted Griffen. But Sam stayed silent. He watched with

amusement. The other owners allowed the rest of the dogs to join in the fun. It was impossible for the workmen to carry on. They couldn't cut trees down with dogs running around them, so they had to give up.

"You wait!" shouted Ted Griffen. "You think you've stopped us. But you haven't. When this park belongs to me, there'll be a big sign on that gate that says 'Keep Out'. And that'll mean you." He pointed at the dogs and glared at Jake in particular.

The workmen packed up all their equipment and left the park.

"He's right of course," said Mr Grant. "We've won today but he'll be back. We have to find a way of stopping that man."

After supper that night, Jake pushed through the fence to Sam's garden. Sam was enjoying a cup of tea in the garden before he turned in for the night.

"Hallo Jake. Well, old boy, what are we going to do? Where am I going to take you to play football? It looks like we're going to lose the park."

"Not if I can help it," thought Jake. "There must be something I can do."

Chapter Five

Next day, Sam went to visit Mr and Mrs Foster. As the Charter could not be found, they needed to find another way of saving the park.

"I wonder how much the park is being sold for," said Mrs Foster. "Perhaps the people of the town could raise the money and buy it, instead of Ted Griffen."

"Well," said Mr Foster, "we would be buying something that already belongs to us. But if it's the only way to save the park, then perhaps we should try."

Mrs Foster telephoned the Town Hall to find out just how much money the park was being sold for. She was surprised to hear that it was less than she thought. The Council needed money quickly. She was told that if the townsfolk could pay as much as Ted Griffen, they could buy the park and it would be saved.

"Then there's hope," said Sam.

"It's still a lot of money to find," said Mr Foster.

"I know," said Mrs Foster, "but we must try. We need to get some people together and think of ideas. I'll start up a fund-raising committee at once. We haven't any time to lose."

Mrs Foster organised a meeting for everybody interested in saving the park. The Fosters' house was packed out. Jake loved it. He liked meeting new people.

People came up with lots of ideas. There would be a sponsored walk, a fun run and a sponsored swim. Jake liked the sound of the walk and the fun run but he wasn't keen on the swim. It seemed too much like a bath.

Mr Grant was put in charge of writing to local businesses to ask them for money. They wouldn't want big, new businesses opening near them.

The main event would be a Grand Fair. There would be lots of side shows and attractions. They would ask the Council's permission to hold the Fair in the park.

The next few weeks were very busy. There were lots of preparations to be made.

First there was the sponsored walk. Walkers asked to be sponsored in two ways. They would be paid for the distance they walked and they would be paid for each leg. All the dogs joined in. As they had four legs instead of two, they raised more money than the humans.

The sponsored fun run took place in the park. Owners and dogs ran together. Sam provided the drinks for the runners. Jake didn't always run in the right direction because there were so many squirrels and rabbits to chase, but he did have fun.

Organising the Fair was a very big job. There needed to be lots of things for people to spend their money on. The park would be full of attractions, things to do and goodies to buy and eat. Posters were put up all round the town to advertise it.

The day before the Fair, everybody was hard at work preparing. They put up flags and balloons and laid out all the stalls and attractions.

"Let's hope we have good weather tomorrow," said Mrs Thirkettle. "We've done all we can."

Chapter Six

The day of the Fair dawned. A few early clouds soon cleared. It was going to be a lovely sunny day. Everyone was relieved. They hoped that all their hard work would be rewarded.

Mr and Mrs Foster and Sam arrived at the park early. Before the Fair started, Jake was allowed to wander round by himself, looking at all the attractions.

In one corner, there was a small fun fair, with a carousel of painted horses, a big wheel and a helter skelter.

On the lake, there were remote control

boats. The ducks were not too sure about them and retreated to the safety of the reeds.

Jake liked the look of the cake stall. He would visit that later!

There were two bouncy castles. Jake tried to have a bounce on one but was chased off because of his sharp claws.

Soon it was time to open the park gates so that the Fair could begin. Mrs Thirkettle cut the red ribbon stretched across the entrance, the local brass band began to play and the fun started.

By the gates there was a shooting range and a coconut shy and next to that, a crockery smash. Jake wondered why it was that people were allowed to make such an awful mess. He was always being told off for breaking much less.

There was lots of food to eat. Candy floss and toffee apples were on sale. Jake tried some candy floss that had fallen off a stick. Unusually for Jake, he thought it was too sweet and it got wrapped round his teeth. But he did like a toffee apple that a little boy gave him.

There was a hot dog and burger stall. This was popular, especially with the

dogs, who were very quick to pick up any dropped burgers. Jake went back to the cake stall. He'd noticed there was a whole tray of home-made chocolates on it. When nobody was looking, he nudged the tray and the chocolates fell on the ground. They were delicious!

Mr Grant had set himself up as a human jukebox. He stood inside a big cardboard box, painted to look like a jukebox. Pasted onto the front was a long list of songs which he could sing. People paid him to sing the song of their choice. Mr Grant's singing was enthusiastic but Mr Foster, on the next stall, wished it was slightly more tuneful. After listening to Mr Grant's efforts for nearly an hour, he paid him to be quiet for five minutes' peace.

Because of his footballing skills, Jake was given a stall to himself. Mr Foster had set up goal posts and measured out an area where people could shoot. Sam held Jake until Mr Foster said "Go", then the competitor tried to score a goal past Jake. Amazingly, only one goal was scored and that was by a little boy who had dropped his ice cream just as he was going to shoot. Instead of going for the ball, Jake went for the ice cream. Jake was kept busy all afternoon. He was exhausted by the end but he'd raised a lot of money and thoroughly enjoyed himself.

All the dogs from the park played their part. A Bernese Mountain dog was harnessed to a little cart and spent the afternoon giving children rides. Charles marched up and down in his father's regimental regalia and collected donations of money in a pot strapped to his back. Even Holly and Harry did their party piece: they shook hands with people.

At the end of the day, Mr and Mrs Foster and Sam counted the money. They had all the money from the Fair, collections, sponsored events and some very generous donations from local businesses, but they were dismayed to find that they still didn't have enough money to buy the park.

There was one last chance. Mr Grant said that one business in the town, Technicom, might give them the amount they needed. But their directors had still not decided.

Everybody was very worried. Even after all their hard work they might not manage to meet the Council's deadline. They only had another couple of days left.

Next day, Sam and the Fosters talked about the problem.

"We haven't raised enough money so,

at the moment, there is nothing to stop Ted Griffen buying the park on Monday. That means tomorrow's the last day we can visit the park." said Mr Foster. "Sam, we'd like to come with you and Jake tomorrow. It'll be the last time for all of us."

Tears welled up in Sam's eyes. "I don't like to think about it," he said. "A walk in the park with Jake is the highlight of my day."

Jake sat next to Sam and gently put his paw on Sam's knee. Even if they couldn't go to the park together, Sam would always be Jake's favourite person.

Chapter Seven

Next day, Mr and Mrs Foster, Sam, Mrs Thirkettle, Jake, Holly and Harry set out for the park together.

When they arrived, they were dismayed to find that the park had already been closed off to the public, and the lovely old park gates were barricaded. Angry locals were gathered around the entrance and all the dogs were looking very agitated.

Fierce-looking barbed wire and steel

girders reinforced the barricades on top of the park fence.

"This is disgraceful," said Mr Grant. "The park won't be sold until tomorrow. They've no right to do this."

"Yes, this is very unfair. The park still belongs to the town until tomorrow," said Mr Foster.

The portly figure of Ted Griffen appeared behind the barricades.

"Ladies and gentlemen, the Council has given permission for the site to be prepared today, so that construction can start tomorrow," he said.

"It's not a site, it's our park!" shouted Sam.

"That's tough," said Ted Griffen. "Let's face it. You've lost. There's no Charter, the park is mine now, and there's nothing you can do about it."

Sam and Jake turned away from the

park gates for the last time.

"Well, boy, we'll just have to walk on the common," Sam said, and the other dogs and their owners joined them.

Jake knew what this meant. He would have to stay on the lead and not be allowed to run free. There were sheep on the common. Dogs had to be kept on leads. They certainly couldn't play football.

The smell of the sheep on the common reminded Jake of the sheep's bone he thought they were looking for, which would save the park.

"It's a pity that Charter bone thing hasn't turned up. Who would have thought a bone could make so much difference?" Jake thought to himself.

Everybody went home feeling very sad. Their last trip to the park had been ruined.

"Well, that's it." said Mr Foster. "We haven't enough money to buy the park, so now it is lost."

Chapter Eight

On Monday, Jake was woken very early by the telephone ringing.

Mrs Foster answered it. "Yes, that's right," she said. "Yes. Really? Well that's wonderful news, thanks so much for letting me know so quickly. Yes, we'll meet you at the Town Hall at ten o'clock."

Mrs Foster put the telephone back and told Mr Foster about the message. Mr

Grant had telephoned. Technicom had sent him a cheque for the rest of the money they needed. Now they could offer as much money as Ted Griffen. The townsfolk could buy the park after all!

Jake rushed out to tell Holly, Harry and Charles.

Everyone was feeling very excited.

The Fosters, Sam and Mrs Thirkettle gathered all the money together. The deadline was eleven o'clock, so they were going to the Town Hall an hour early to give the Council the money. To his disgust, Jake was brushed thoroughly and made to look smart.

"Have to look your best for the presentation, Jake," said Mrs Foster, trying to make him keep still. "Now, stand up, Jake, I can't brush you lying down."

When they were ready, Jake, Sam, the

Fosters and Mrs Thirkettle walked to the Town Hall. Mr Grant was waiting for them and handed over the money from Technicom.

Ted Griffen was also waiting to see the Mayor. He was shown into the Mayor's office first.

After a short time, Jake's group were asked into the office. The Mayor was standing with Ted Griffen, who was wearing a smug grin.

The Mayor's office was very large and lavishly decorated. The furniture looked new and expensive with several beautiful paintings hanging on the walls. In pride of place, there was a large and very old painting of the park, showing the beautiful trees that Ted Griffen's men were now cutting down.

Mrs Foster stepped forward. "Mr Mayor, I'm very pleased to tell you that the people of the town have managed to raise the same amount as Mr Griffen, and so, on their behalf, I'd like to make an offer to buy the park," she said.

For an awkward moment, the Mayor was silent. "Oh dear," he said at last. "Oh dear, you see, I'm afraid that's not possible."

Mrs Foster looked puzzled. "Why ever not?" she said. "You told us that the Council would sell the park to us if we raised as much as Ted Griffen has offered."

"Well, that's just it, I'm afraid," said the Mayor. "Mr Griffen has just offered me twice as much as before. My duty to the Council is to sell the park to the highest bidder."

"What about your duty to the people of the town?" shouted Mr Grant. "This is outrageous!"

Everybody started shouting. The Mayor panicked and called for his security guards to throw them all out.

"You can't do this," said Mr Foster. "You must listen to us. It's our park." And he began to struggle with a security guard who had taken hold of his arm.

Suddenly, things happened very quickly. A table was knocked over, which sent a large pot plant flying. As the plant fell, it knocked the painting of the park off the wall. The painting crashed onto a filing cabinet and ended up on the floor. The frame was damaged and the canvas was ripped open.

"Now look what you've done!" shouted the Mayor. "That painting is extremely valuable, more valuable than you could possibly know." He rushed to get hold of the painting but Jake got there first.

Jake scratched at the ripped canvas and made it even worse. "Look at what your dreadful dog is doing," yelled the Mayor. "Stop him. He's ruining the painting."

Everybody was horrified. Jake was scratching away frantically.

"Oh Jake," Mrs Foster cried. "What are you doing?"

Sam went to stop Jake, who was, by

now, tearing furiously at the painting. Then something caught Sam's eye. Something was stuck between the canvas and the back of the painting.

Sam looked closer. "All right boy, I can see it. I'll get it now," Sam said to Jake. Carefully he took hold of the painting and out slid an old brown document.

"So, what is this?" he said. He handed it to Mrs Thirkettle. She stared at it for a moment. Then a huge smile spread over her face.

"This, everyone, is the Royal Charter," she said, "which gives the parkland to the people of this town 'in perpetuity'. That means for ever. It says here that the land must always be a park for the town 'by order of King Edward'."

"Hurrah!" said Mrs Foster. "So the park isn't yours to sell," she said to the

Mayor, "and you can't buy it!" she said to Ted Griffen.

"Just a minute," said Mr Grant, "I hope you didn't know the Charter was in that painting, Mr Mayor."

The Mayor just sat red-faced at his desk, his eyes bulging, unable to speak.

"Well done, Jake!" said Sam. "You've saved the day. I think you could smell the Charter, couldn't you boy?"

"Yes, well done, Jake!" said Mrs Foster. "What a good job you came with us." And everybody, except the Mayor and Ted Griffen, made a big fuss of Jake.

As soon as the painting had ripped, Jake recognised the smell. It was the same as the sheep on the common.

"Sheepskin, not sheep's bone!" thought Jake.

Chapter Nine

Thanks to Jake, the park was safe. The Charter was put in a very secure place by the townsfolk in a vault in the main bank. Ted Griffen and his men were made to take down the barricades at the park and plant new trees for any they had cut down. The councillors were dismissed and made to sell their cars. The rest of the paintings and the antiques were sold.

The townsfolk used the money they had raised to improve the park. They planted some more trees, put in new swings and roundabouts, renovated the bandstand and did many of the jobs the Council should have done but hadn't.

There was still some money left, so, to celebrate, they held a slap-up picnic in the park, in Jake's honour.

Jake had a wonderful time. There were lots of games to play and food to eat, including a cake made out of chocolate.

Best of all, Jake was allowed to play football with the local team on the big football pitch.

Tired but happy, Jake walked home with Sam and the gang.

"Jake," said Sam, "thanks to you, one

of my favourite places has been saved. Thank you." And he gave Jake a big hug.

That night, Jake was pottering around the garden when he smelt it. Bonemeal. Mr Foster had planted some bulbs, and he had used bonemeal.

Jake was about to dig them up, when a voice called out behind him. "Jake, what are you doing?" Mr Foster was standing at the back door.

Jake turned and trotted back to the house.

"Just checking," he said to himself.

Jake in Trouble

Chapter One

Jake was excited. He was going on holiday to a farm.

Jake had never been on holiday before and he had never been to a farm.

He was looking forward to meeting all the animals. He knew there were sheep on the farm because he'd heard his owners, Mr and Mrs Foster, telling Sam.

Sam was Jake's favourite person. He lived in the house at the bottom of Jake's garden. Sam took Jake for walks in their local park. He always had a friendly word and pat for Jake. Jake usually stayed with Sam when the Fosters went on holiday. But this year, they were all going together.

Of course, Jake would miss his friends from the park, especially Holly, the collie, who lived next door. Jake told her how excited he was. He was especially looking forward to herding some sheep.

Holly didn't think he'd be allowed to do that. Farmers were very funny about their sheep. They were fussy about dogs. She'd even heard of a dog being shot at because he was in a field with sheep.

Jake found that hard to believe and thought Holly was just being silly. He was sure he'd be able to do it. Jake reminded Holly that his grandfather was a Belgian Shepherd dog, so he had sheep herding in his blood.

Holly looked doubtful. She said that

even though she was a Rough Collie, with lots of herding "in her blood", she wouldn't want to try and push big sheep about.

Jake wasn't worried. He was going to have a great time, and when he returned from holiday, he would tell her all about it.

Chapter Two

Jake was prepared for a long journey to the farm. He settled down in the back of the car.

He was right. It was a long way. He must have had eight sleeps! This was the longest journey he'd ever had and he was glad to jump out of the car into the farmyard.

The farmer's wife, Mrs Warden, greeted them and began to explain where the Fosters and Sam would find the caravans. Nobody noticed what Jake was doing.

He had spotted some farmyard ducks nesting in a corner, by a big barn. They were a different colour to the ducks in the park, but Jake was sure they'd be ready for a game.

He charged towards the ducks, expecting them to complain noisily at him, ruffle their feathers a bit and then settle back down onto their nests.

But these ducks didn't. They weren't used to boisterous dogs and they ran out of the farmyard, leaving their nests and their eggs to go cold.

Jake was surprised. The farmer's wife was very annoyed.

"I'm terribly sorry, Mrs Warden. He's used to chasing the ducks in the park." Mrs Foster said.

Mrs Warden looked at the eggs and

sighed. "Well, it can't be helped." she said. "He's had a long journey, so he's probably full of beans. But it might be best if you keep him on a lead around the farmyard. My husband doesn't like dogs who can't behave themselves."

At that moment, Mr Warden arrived in the farmyard with his sheepdog, who was called Shep.

Shep was a working sheepdog, and had herded sheep all his life. He was wary of town dogs. He thought they were stupid.

Eagerly, Jake ran to him, ready to introduce himself and make friends. But Shep walked straight past and ignored him.

Jake felt quite upset. He liked to be friends and he didn't care if his friends were clever or not, he liked them anyway. But this Shep seemed a very unfriendly dog.

The Fosters and Sam drove over to the field where their caravans were sited. There were only two so it was a peaceful spot. Jake was to stay in Sam's caravan because there would be more room.

The caravans were next to a field with sheep in. "That's good," thought Jake. "I'll probably get a chance to herd them. That'll show Shep I'm not completely stupid!"

Chapter Three

The next day started bright and early for the farm. Mr Warden was taking Shep to a local sheepdog trial. The sheepdogs would all compete against one another to see who was the best at herding sheep.

Everybody was very excited. Last year, they had come second, but this year Mr Warden was hoping to bring back the lovely silver cup awarded as first prize. He thought Shep was the best sheepdog he'd ever had.

Jake felt a bit jealous. He knew he had done a few useful things but it wasn't the same as working, like Shep.

The Fosters and Sam were invited along and they were all looking forward to it. Jake liked the look of the ham sandwiches they prepared for their picnic. He hoped he might get a bite of one later.

There was a short journey to the trial. It was being held in the grounds of a lovely old stately home. Mrs Foster was keen to look round it later, if possible.

When they arrived, the Fosters and Sam unpacked their chairs and picnic. They found themselves a good spot for watching the competition and settled down to enjoy the day.

Jake wasn't enjoying himself very

much at all. While other dogs seemed to be having a wonderful time, chasing sheep, he was tied up to Sam's deck chair.

"Oh well," he thought, "at least if I watch carefully, I might pick up a few tips. Then I can have a go myself."

This herding business looked easy. The sheep seemed a dull lot. The shepherd was doing a lot of whistling while the sheepdog raced up the field, collected a group of sheep and brought them back to the shepherd.

Jake wasn't impressed. He thought that by the end of the afternoon the sheep should know the way by themselves.

Some dogs were better than others. One unfortunate shepherd was herded into the pen with the sheep by his dog. He was squashed by the sheep against the side of the pen and another shepherd had to help him get out.

But the star of the day was Shep. Even Jake had to admit that he did a superb job. The sheep did exactly what they should do and Mr Warden and Shep had them in the sheep pen in record time. Shep seemed really happy when he was herding the sheep.

"I wish he was a bit friendlier," Jake thought. "We could be good friends."

Mr Warden came over to speak to the Fosters and Sam. Jake congratulated Shep. But Shep stuck his nose in the air and ignored him.

The results were read out. Mr Warden and Shep had won easily. The beautiful trophy, with the silver statue of a sheepdog on the top, was awarded to them, to keep for a year.

On the way back to the farm, Jake thought how nice it would be to prove to Shep that he wasn't the only one who could do useful things. Tomorrow, he would look for a chance to show that he could herd sheep as well.

"Nothing to it," thought Jake. "Easy."

Chapter Four

The next day, the Fosters and Sam decided to have a very early breakfast and then spend the day on a long walk. Jake was looking forward to it. He loved a good walk. There were lots of new smells here and there might even be some rabbits to chase.

The Fosters kept Jake on his lead as they walked through the farmyard. Shep, the collie, was lying down, waiting for the farmer to start work. He had a lot of sheep to move from one field to another and it was going to be a busy day. Jake said hallo to him but Shep ignored him.

"I'm not talking to that idiot of a dog," thought Shep.

Jake was sad. "I'll show him," he thought.

Jake liked to lead the way when he was set free and once they had left the farmyard behind, Mrs Foster let him loose. The countryside was an ideal place for Jake to run in. It was an interesting walk, with mounds of rock to investigate and lots of trees to sniff at. The Fosters and Sam enjoyed the views and Sam spotted a rare bird that he'd never seen before. Jake was fed up because he had to sit still until the bird flew off.

They walked until midday when they stopped to eat their packed lunch. Jake had a drink of water and a dog biscuit. The Fosters and Sam were tired after their lunch and they all dozed off, lying in the sunshine.

Jake didn't think much of this. They were picnicking in a field with lots of interesting dips and lumps and bumps in it, so Jake decided to explore.

He discovered some exciting smells and found some fox's dung to roll in. Behind a gorse bush, he disturbed a rabbit. The rabbit rushed off and Jake chased after it. They ran round and round the field until the rabbit disappeared behind another bush.

Jake rushed over to follow it. Suddenly, he stopped. Danger. Jake could sense danger. It seemed as if the ground was not safe. It felt odd. It might even give way.

He stood still. He could feel the ground moving under his paws. He crouched low, and slowly turned round. He crawled back the way he had come until he felt the ground was safe again. He didn't like it at all and wondered what it was.

By now, the Fosters and Sam were waking up.

"Well, what do you think? Shall we go on or shall we head back?" said Mr Foster. They all agreed to go back to the farm.

For once, Jake wasn't sorry. He didn't want to stay in this field.

The party packed up and headed for home. They walked slower than in the morning and Jake was getting a bit impatient to be moving on.

They were quite close to the farm when Jake heard the farmer's sheep bleating in their new field. Jake was in front of the Fosters and Sam. He looked back at them, and then, without warning, he dashed off towards the field of sheep.

The Fosters were taken by surprise. They called Jake who seemed to have suddenly become deaf.

"I bet he's going after those sheep," said Mr Foster. "We'd better hurry up and catch him. Farmers can shoot at dogs that worry sheep."

They ran after Jake, but Jake had a big start on them, and he was much faster. He reached the field of sheep and looked for a hole in the fence. Finding a small one, he squeezed through it. The sheep ignored him and carried on grazing.

"Well, what now?" thought Jake. "I'll try to get them together in a group. That's what I need to do."

The sheep were scattered about the

field. He ran up to each sheep but they ignored him. One even chased him away.

"Right," thought Jake. "I know what will get them going," and he went up to a very big sheep and nipped its leg.

The sheep was furious. She rounded on Jake and chased him all over the field. The rest of the sheep started a huge commotion, cheering her on and barging each other out of the way.

Mr Warden heard the noise back at the farmhouse. He thought it must be a fox worrying his sheep. As he ran out of the farmhouse door, he was carrying his shotgun.

He ran up to the field. Jake heard a loud click. Then a bang. Jake was terrified. He fled to the fence and tried to find the hole. He couldn't. He started to panic. Frantically he ran up and down. Then something stung his ear. Jake whimpered. He'd been hit.

Another shot came whistling past his head.

The hole? Where was it?

Just as he had given up hope, there it was. At that moment, Mr Warden recognised Jake. He was livid. Sam and Mrs Foster came running up.

"Mr Warden, I'm terribly sorry. I don't know what's got into Jake. I'm so sorry," she said.

"Mrs Foster, you have to keep him away from my animals. He's a danger to them, and to himself," Mr Warden said. "I could have killed him."

Mrs Foster grabbed hold of Jake and yanked him by his collar. Jake thought she was going to strangle him.

Jake couldn't believe it – after all he had suffered, this was the treatment he was getting.

"You bad dog, Jake. You're lucky to be alive," Mrs Foster said.

Jake didn't feel very lucky at that moment.

Sam looked anxiously at him. He didn't agree with shooting. He felt Jake all over to check he had not been hurt.

Now Mr Foster had arrived. In his hurry to get to Jake, he had fallen badly and sprained his wrist. He was nursing his painful arm, and assured Mr Warden that Jake would get into no more trouble.

Back at the farmyard, Shep sneered at Jake. Herding sheep was a difficult job, needing expert dogs like him, not idiot town dogs like Jake. And then he turned his back on Jake and said no more to him.

Jake was thoroughly miserable. He'd been very frightened. He could have been killed. He was in disgrace, and he felt a failure. Far from being able to herd sheep, they had ignored him, then chased him and laughed at him. Shep had jeered at him and, worst of all, Mr Foster had sprained his wrist.

The Fosters and Sam returned to their caravans, and they all agreed that they would have to keep a very close eye on Jake. He mustn't be allowed to run around loose anymore, certainly not near the sheep.

Oh no! Jake knew that this would mean he would be tied up all the time.

After Sam had given him his supper, he disappeared under the bed and stayed there until the morning, sulking.

Chapter Five

The next day, the Fosters and Sam wanted to visit the museum in the local town.

There was, however, a problem with Jake. He couldn't go with them to the museum – dogs weren't allowed – and the caravan was too small to leave him in all day.

"I know," said Mrs Warden, "he can stay in the barn for the day. He can't come to any harm in there. It's very big and fairly empty at the moment. There's only old Rudi in there."

Mrs Warden was a kind-hearted lady and she felt sorry for Jake. She gave him a bone to chew on as he was led into the barn.

Rudi was a big, fat, old pig. She had been a very good pig for the Wardens, who spoilt her now. She was allowed the barn to herself. Being a mother was what she did best and she had produced lots of healthy piglets. Rudi beamed a great motherly smile at Jake and introduced herself.

Jake liked her straight away. She was the first friendly face he had found on the farm. He loved the smell of Rudi and the cosiness of her sty. She had her bed, made of straw, in one corner of the barn and she invited Jake over to the corner for a chat.

It wasn't long before the whole sorry tale of Jake's visit came out. Jake told her that he couldn't understand why the sheep wouldn't do as he wanted.

Rudi told him that sheep are really very stubborn. They only do what they want to do. They obeyed Shep because the farmer was there with him. Shep thinks he's in charge, but he's not.

Jake had to disagree with her. He thought Shep definitely knew what he was doing with sheep.

Jake asked Rudi if she had any idea why Shep was so horrible to him. Rudi told him that Shep was a very proud dog and he had no close friends, even on the farm. He didn't think anybody was as clever as him and he was rather a lonely dog.

Rudi said that Shep was very wary of strangers. But she was sure that he would like Jake as a friend. She could tell Jake was a lively dog who enjoyed himself. Shep always concentrated on only one thing, which meant he couldn't sense danger and was easily taken by surprise. He wouldn't be any good in a town. Rudi was sure Jake could teach Shep a thing or two, even if it wasn't how to herd sheep!

Jake was sure Shep would never listen to a word he said.

Jake chatted about all his town friends, how together they had saved their local park. He was very modest. He didn't tell Rudi that he was the one that had saved it. He told her about his visit to Crufts Dog Show and how wonderful it was.

And he talked about Sam, his friend, who was always on his side. He told her about their football games together every day, in the local park. Jake loved football and he was very good at it. He chatted about Holly and how much he missed his friends from the park.

This made him even more sad and he slumped down on the floor, his ears down, feeling very low.

Rudi tried to cheer Jake up. She wondered if he would like some of her potato peelings. Of all the leftovers given to her each day, she saved the peelings to eat as a special treat. But Jake could have them today. Rudi believed that most problems could be solved by something tasty to eat.

Jake looked at them. He usually had a huge appetite but even he drew the line at raw potato peelings.

He appreciated the thought, but politely turned down the offer. Rudi didn't need much persuasion and ate the peelings whilst trying to cheer Jake up. She was sure that Shep would change his mind about Jake. Jake was obviously a very clever dog.

Jake appreciated Rudi's efforts. He was glad to have found at least one friend on the farm. But he didn't think Shep would ever change his mind.

Chapter Six

Sam was worried about Jake. He thought Jake was missing his pals, and of course, he was right.

Sam wanted to cheer Jake up. He usually played football with him, but since the shooting, he didn't think it was safe to let him off the lead around the farm.

Sam remembered that he had seen a big park nearby. He asked the Fosters if he could take Jake there.

"That would be lovely, Sam. Why don't you borrow the car and drive there?" Mrs Foster said. "Do you mind if we stay here? I think John needs to rest. His wrist is very swollen."

"That's fine. And we don't need the car, thank you. Jake and I can walk there," Sam replied.

Jake was very pleased to be going somewhere just with Sam, especially as Sam had the football bag in his hand. Trotting along the country lanes at Sam's side, he thought perhaps things weren't so bad after all.

As they approached the park, Sam was surprised to see so many people. A big banner was stretched across the entrance, saying "Country Fair".

A large arena had been set up. In the centre, there was a big circle with a stage in the middle and seats all around it. The rest of the arena was filled with stalls selling all kinds of goods: cheeses, jams, cakes, sausages, baskets, candles, leather goods. Jake thought he could see some chocolates. He hoped they could visit the stalls after their game.

Sam and Jake had a long and lively game of football. Jake felt like he'd been let out of prison. He threw himself at the football. He headed the ball eight times on the trot, which was a record for him.

"Bet Shep can't do this!" he thought.

After their game, Jake and Sam returned to the Country Fair. It was very busy.

There were crowds of people bustling around the stalls. Jake was disappointed to see that the chocolate stall was very busy and nearly all the chocolates had been sold. He did manage to eat a sample piece of cheese that had fallen off the cheese stall and he thought it was very nice.

When they reached the arena, Sam spotted a spare seat near the front, so he sat down to watch.

A group of men came into the arena. Jake had never seen anyone dressed like them before. They had ribbons all over them, even on their feet, and some jingling brass bells tied to their shoes. They were carrying big thick sticks which also had ribbons tied to them. To Jake's amazement, they started running round the circle, ringing their bells and bashing their sticks together.

Jake didn't like the sticks. They looked like they could really hurt. He started to growl.

"It's alright, boy," Sam said. "They're only Morris dancers."

At that moment, the men came close to Sam and nearly hit him. This was too much for Jake. He jumped up and rushed into the middle of them, trying to get their sticks, barking loudly. The Morris dancers tried to catch him, so they could finish their dance. Unfortunately, one of the Morris Men got tangled up in his own ribbons and fell over. His stick fell from his hand. Jake grabbed hold of it and rushed over to Sam.

Sam took Jake by the collar and retrieved the stick. As he gave it back to the Morris Man he said how sorry he was.

But the Morris Men were not cross at all. They were laughing heartily. In fact, they thought Jake had added something to their performance. He had certainly livened things up. The audience loved it too. They thought Jake was a part of the act.

Sam decided to take Jake back to the farm quickly, before he could get into any more mischief. He was very relieved that the Morris dancers had been so nice.

As Sam and Jake arrived at the farmyard, Mr Warden was standing at the farmhouse door, looking very worried.

"What's wrong?" asked Sam.

"It's Shep," replied Mr Warden, "he's gone missing. This morning, I was getting ready to check on the sheep. I whistled for Shep, but he didn't come. He is not on the farm. It's not like Shep to stray, he can always find his way back. We've looked everywhere on the farm and now I'm wondering if he's been stolen. He's a prize-winning sheepdog, and there's lots of folks would want him."

"Perhaps you should search further afield," suggested Sam.

"We'll have to," replied Mr Warden, "But it's not like Shep to leave the farm."

Sam returned to the caravans and told the Fosters. "They're going to organise a search party to look for him," he said.

"He's probably been stolen," thought Jake. "Now, if I could only find him, and the thief. They wouldn't call me a useless town dog then."

But Jake didn't get a chance to look. The next day, he watched the search party set out.

He stayed tied up outside the caravan. Lots of people turned out. Shep was well known, and Mr Warden had offered a generous reward.

Jake heard Mr Warden tell the people where they were going to search. They would look tomorrow as well if they had to.

"I wish I could go with them," Jake thought. But, since the shooting, the Fosters and Sam hadn't let Jake out of their sight.

Much later, the search party returned, with still no sign of Shep. It began to look as if he had been stolen.

Chapter Seven

The next morning, the search party set off again to look for Shep. By the afternoon, they had still not returned, and nor had Shep.

The Fosters and Sam were preparing their evening meal. They were all inside the Fosters' caravan. Jake was tied to a post outside. His lead was looped over the top. He started to chew at it, then he pulled at it, but it was a very strong lead and he couldn't break it.

Then Jake had an idea. Slowly, he started to push the lead up the post.

It was nearly at the top when Sam came out of the caravan to peel some potatoes in the sunshine. Jake sat still immediately and hoped that Sam didn't notice the lead was nearly at the top of the post. Eventually Sam went back into the caravan and Jake carried on pushing the lead until it reached the top of the post. Then, it slipped off. Jake was free.

He ran off with the lead trailing behind him.

Some time later, when Sam and the Fosters had finished eating, they noticed Jake had gone. They were frantic. Jake would get himself killed this time. They called and called but he was already a long way away.

Jake didn't have any plan of how to find Shep. He wanted to find a clue or a fresh smell that might help him. He ran for a long time, to make sure the Fosters wouldn't follow him. Then he realised he was getting near the field that he didn't like, the field where he had sensed danger.

Jake stopped quickly. He wasn't going to risk that field.

Then he smelt something. It was not a smell that people would recognise, but one that animals know well. Fear. It was the smell of something, or someone, who is afraid. Carefully, Jake crawled into the field and the smell got stronger. The closer Jake got to danger, the stronger the smell was getting.

Then Jake knew what he could smell. He could smell Shep. And Shep was frightened. But Jake couldn't see him anywhere.

What should he do? He could sense great danger all around him.

He should turn back.

But Jake couldn't turn back. Shep needed his help, wherever he was. And Jake bravely carried on, crawling through the field.

Just as the smell was at its strongest, and the danger felt unbearable, Jake saw it. The ground had fallen away right in front of him and there was a small hole, just big enough for a dog to fall through.

Jake listened. He could hear something faint but unmistakable. It was the sound of a dog whimpering.

When he dared to look down the hole, it was very dark. Eventually, his eyes got used to it and then he could see that the hole was very deep. As he looked, he thought he could see a little shape on a narrow ledge halfway down.

He called. The little shape moved and howled back at him.

It was Shep! He was so pleased to see Jake. He had been so stupid. He'd raced after a rabbit and ended up falling down here.

Shep's pleasure at seeing Jake high above him soon faded when he realised that Jake couldn't get him out. Shep had hurt his leg badly and he couldn't move from the little ledge. He would fall further down the deep hole. He had no food but luckily, there was water dripping past him and he could drink that.

But both dogs realised that unless Jake could get help, Shep wasn't going to survive.

Jake didn't know what he was going to do. He wasn't allowed to be off the lead around the farm, and after this, he would be watched even more closely.

Shep went very quiet. Jake reassured him that he would do whatever he could to get him rescued. Jake would find a way. He must.

The Fosters were furious with Jake when he returned to the farm.

"We'll have to keep him shut up most of the time now," Mr Foster said.

"At least he's come back," Sam said. He was very pleased to see Jake.

Jake prowled up and down. He was very restless and he wouldn't eat his food. He couldn't sit still and kept pulling at Sam's clothes and crying at the door.

He couldn't make them understand.

Jake was really worried. He didn't mind for himself. He didn't mind so much if he was kept shut up, especially if he had Rudi for company.

But he was very worried for Shep. He knew that if he didn't get help very soon, Shep wouldn't last out much longer on that little ledge.

Chapter Eight

The next day, the Fosters and Sam needed to buy some food. So Jake was left in the barn, with Rudi. Jake hurriedly told her all about Shep.

Rudi was pleased Jake had found Shep. She said how clever he'd been.

Jake didn't feel very clever. He couldn't think of a way to rescue Shep. There was no point being clever enough to find him, without being able to rescue him.

Rudi knew that the search party was

going out for the last time, today. She thought that Jake should try and get them to follow him, so he could lead them to Shep. They'd try to catch Jake at least, wouldn't they, after all the fuss with the sheep.

Jake needed to find a way out of the barn, which seemed impossible.

He looked at the big door. It was bolted on the outside. No way of opening that. He noticed that the door handle was like the one on the back door at home. He could let himself in at home by jumping up and pulling the handle down. The barn door opened outwards, so if it didn't have a bolt on the outside, Jake was sure he could just pull down the handle and push the door open.

But there was a bolt, and even as Jake told Rudi, he knew it was no good.

Then Rudi had an idea. Dear old

Rudi, who usually only worried about her next meal. But it was thinking about her breakfast that gave Rudi her idea.

Rudi whispered her plan to Jake. Mrs Warden would be along soon, with Rudi's breakfast, leftovers from the farm. She would have to unbolt the door to get into the barn. She would shut it behind her but, if Jake was quick, he could open the door and rush away before she noticed. Rudi would do her best to distract her and give Jake more time.

Jake thought it was a brilliant plan. Rudi blushed.

Mrs Warden arrived with the breakfast. At that moment, Rudi began to moan, as if she had stomach pains.

"What is it, old girl? Not feeling yourself this morning? Perhaps I'd better not give you this," Mrs Warden said.

Rudi stopped groaning straight away.

She wanted to help, but she also wanted her breakfast.

But this gave Jake just enough time and while Mrs Warden wasn't looking, he leaped up at the door, pulled down the handle and ran out of the barn into the farmyard.

The search party was just preparing to leave. Jake rushed around them, barking loudly to get their attention.

When Mr Warden realised who it was, he shouted, "Quickly, catch him quickly!

He'll get himself lost next. Get that dog back in the barn."

Jake ran backwards and forwards. He wanted people to follow him, but he couldn't let them catch him. It was very tricky and it took all his skill to weave in and out without being caught.

The farmyard was in uproar. Geese and ducks were flapping all over the place. People were falling over them and one another as they tried to catch Jake.

Jake's idea was to lead them out of the farmyard. They followed him a little way but then they gave up.

This was no good at all. This was not what Jake had in mind. He'd escaped from the barn but he couldn't get the search party to follow him. Everything had gone wrong. What could he do?

Jake decided that at least he could check if Shep was still alive.

When he came to the field, he crawled carefully to the hole and looked down to see Shep, still stuck on the little ledge. Shep was very pleased to see Jake again but he was disappointed that Jake hadn't managed to get the rescuers to follow him.

Jake chatted for a long time to Shep, trying to cheer him up. Shep was feeling very cold and damp, and extremely hungry. He was beginning to give up hope of being rescued.

As he lay carefully at the top of the hole, Jake suddenly caught sight of something glinting. It was a little way down, and Jake had to be very careful as he tried to see what it was.

Then Jake recognised it. It was a small metal disc, like he and all his friends had attached to their collars. Jake realised he was looking at Shep's name tag. It had come off his collar as he had fallen.

Then Jake had an idea.

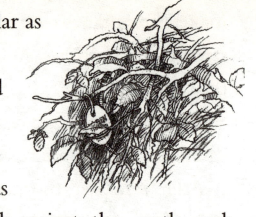

Carefully, Jake pressed himself as flat as he could against the earth and slowly leaned forward.

It was very scary. Jake found himself looking down into the big black hole. One sudden movement and he would find himself down there with Shep, or perhaps falling past him into the blackness.

Slowly, he reached forward and grabbed the metal disc in his mouth. But, as he did, the earth started to crumble away beneath him. He stopped dead. He was perched at the top of the hole, with the disc in his mouth.

He couldn't move. When he tried to

make the smallest movement, the earth started to fall into the hole again, threatening to take him with it.

He stayed still for a very long time. He didn't dare shout down to Shep.

After what seemed like ages, Jake knew he had to risk moving. He couldn't stay there.

Slowly, little by little, he moved first one part of his leg, then another, back from the mouth of the hole. Beneath him, lumps of mud and stones fell into the mine. He had to force himself to be patient and move very slowly, something he wasn't used to doing.

At long last, he managed to reach safer ground, away from the mouth of the hole. Excitedly, he shouted down to Shep, to tell him he'd managed to get his name tag. Jake explained his plan.

Shep was full of admiration. Jake was

so brave and rather clever. His cleverness was different to Shep's and Shep had to admit there were things Jake could do that he couldn't. Thank goodness!

Jake said goodbye and raced off towards the farm.

Chapter Nine

When Jake got back to the farmyard, the search party had returned and they all looked very sad.

They sat in a circle, drinking tea with the farmer, who thanked them for all their efforts.

"We've tried very hard," Mr Warden said, "but sadly, I have to say, that we'll never see Shep again."

At that moment, Jake rushed into the

middle of the circle. In his enthusiasm, he jumped on top of Mr Warden and nearly knocked him off the straw bale he was sitting on.

"Oh, not you!" Mr Warden said, "Now why couldn't you get lost?"

Then Jake dropped Shep's name tag into Mr Warden's lap and danced around excitedly.

"Mad, completely mad, you are," Mr Warden said.

Then Mrs Warden noticed the tag. "What's that in your lap?" she asked. "What has Jake just dropped?"

Mr Warden picked up the tag and looked at it carefully. Then his face lit up.

"It's Shep's name tag! How did you find it, boy?" he said to Jake.

Jake barked loudly and started to run out of the farmyard. He ran back to Mr

Warden and started to push him with his nose.

"Alright, boy, I get the message," laughed Mr Warden. "You want us to follow you."

At last he had made them understand! Jake rushed out of the farmyard with the rescuers close behind.

When they reached the field, Jake slowed down and started to crawl forward. Jake was very nervous. He didn't want to go back to the hole. The earth around it was ready to collapse.

Mr Warden could see that Jake thought the field was dangerous so he stopped everybody.

"I think I'd better follow Jake alone. It looks like he thinks the ground isn't safe." Mr Warden copied Jake, following him carefully across the field.

Eventually they came to the hole and Jake stopped. He knew that they shouldn't go any nearer.

He barked loudly to let Shep know he'd arrived and that Mr Warden was with him.

Shep barked back, and Mr Warden heard him. "Well, well. It's an old mine shaft. I didn't know this was here. And that's Shep's bark. He must be trapped down there. Oh well done Jake, you clever boy. I have misjudged you. You found Shep and you were clever enough not to fall down yourself."

Mr Warden crept forward to the edge of the hole. He looked down and once his eyes had got used to the gloom, he could see where Shep was stuck.

"Alright, Shep old boy. We'll soon have you out of there."

Shep barked weakly to Mr Warden.

Mr Warden called for two rescuers to help him. They had ropes and equipment, so they could go down the deep hole.

Firstly, they did what they could to make the top safer with some pieces of wood. Then one of them was lowered down into the hole. He made a sling out of Mr Warden's jacket and carefully put Shep inside it. Slowly Shep was pulled up out of the hole.

Shep was pleased to see everybody but he was most pleased to see Jake. He nuzzled at Jake and licked his face, thanking him for rescuing him. He was so sorry that he had been unfriendly.

Jake told him to not to worry. They could be good friends now.

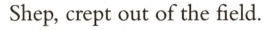

Carefully, Jake and the rescuers carrying Shep, crept out of the field.

They returned to the farm to be met by the Fosters and Sam, who couldn't find Jake in the barn and were worried about what had happened.

They were very relieved to see Jake with Mr Warden and thrilled when the farmer explained how Jake had led them to Shep.

"You've got a grand dog there, Mr Foster," Mr Warden said. "When I first met him, I thought he'd be nothing but trouble. Shows how wrong you can be!"

Mr and Mrs Warden were thrilled to have Shep back. To show their gratitude to Jake they offered the reward money to the Fosters and another week's holiday on the farm. The Fosters and Sam were pleased to accept the extra week but didn't accept the money. Jake had found Shep and money didn't mean anything to Jake. He was just pleased that, at last, Shep was his friend.

Shep had to hop about. He had hurt his leg badly but he was determined to make sure Jake enjoyed the rest of his holiday.

He offered to teach Jake to herd sheep. At first Jake thought this would be very nice. Then he looked across at the big sheep grazing in the field. He thanked Shep very much, but he thought perhaps he'd better leave it to the experts.

Jake had had a lovely holiday. He'd found a new friend in Shep and even made friends with Mr Warden.

Now he was looking forward to going home and telling Holly about his holiday. He would tell her about the rescue. He'd tell her about the Morris Men. He'd tell her about Shep and Rudi the pig.

He would tell Holly all about his adventures. Well, perhaps not quite all.

He might leave out the bit about the sheep